SLOW BLOOMING GRATITUDES

New Women's Voices Series, No. 130

poems by

Sarah W. Bartlett

Finishing Line Press
Georgetown, Kentucky

SLOW BLOOMING GRATITUDES

New Women's Voices Series, No. 130

Copyright © 2017 by Sarah W. Bartlett
ISBN 978-1-63534-199-7 First Edition
All rights reserved under International and Pan-American Copyright Conventions. No part of this book may be reproduced in any manner whatsoever without written permission from the publisher, except in the case of brief quotations embodied in critical articles and reviews.

ACKNOWLEDGMENTS

These poems first appeared in the following publications:

'Equinox' and 'Milkweed,' featured poems in *the Aurorean*, Encircle Publications, Farmington, ME, Fall/Winter 2016.

'Courage and Grace' in 'Body Image' issue of *Minerva Rising*, v.10, April 2016

'Generations' in 'Change' issue of *Mom Egg Review*, v.14, March 2016

'Full Circle' in *SIBLINGS: Our First Macrocosm*, WisingUpPress, GA, 2015

'Hunger' in *Literary Mama*, June 15, 2013

'For Keeps' in 'Beginnings and Ends' issue of *Halfway Down the Stairs*, a quarterly online literary magazine; September 2010.

'Preserving October 1997' in *the Aurorean*, Encircle Publications, Farmington, ME. August 2004

Publisher: Leah Maines
Editor: Christen Kincaid
Cover Art: Anne-Marie Littenberg, annemarielittenberg.com
Author Photo: Jim Hester; jimhestervt.com
Cover Design: Sarah W. Bartlett

Printed in the USA on acid-free paper.
Order online: www.finishinglinepress.com
       also available on amazon.com

Author inquiries and mail orders:
Finishing Line Press
P. O. Box 1626
Georgetown, Kentucky 40324
U. S. A.

Table of Contents

Milkweed 1
Generations 2
Preserving October 1997 3
My Little Guy Has One of His Own.................................. 4
This Small Singer 5
Hunger 7
Pantoum for my Father 8
Courage 9
The Key 10
For Keeps 11
The Return 12
The Moment 13
Full Circle 14
Presence 15
Late Spring... 16
Laughter 17
Fall Song 18
Zen Dog 19
Words the Dog Knows 20
Living with Dying... 21
Seeing Myself for the First Time..................................... 22
Courage and Grace 23
New England Memory 24
She and I 26
Deliberation 27
Discovery 28
Found 29
Equinox 30

MILKWEED

Like milkweed seeds
with their parachutes of silk,
may my words settle
into your heart

their landing unnoticed
'til they root, emerge
into service and sense—thus

I want my words to spread
beauty and use, healing surprise
to calm your breath, your fevered stress,
to purify what circles within

that feeling and thought might open you
to beauty and nurture against bitterness
that would divide; like milkweed,

weave a silken cord connecting
head and heart—yours,
mine and ours.

GENERATIONS

Unabashedly abundant, new growth clematis
spills across the river-side railing, sprouts
up through decking cracks, climbs and twists
tight tendrils about trellis and feeder, purple
flags aflutter effusively eclipsing

worn-to-shreds strips of sturdy old vine
holding steady yet, weathered
from years of climbing, carrying on
the singular task of stringing sturdy structures
to root offshoots in the rich soil of home.

This entwined tangle my dream of family
extended: roots sunk and shoots sprung
from the richness within, weathered fore-vines
supporting the new finding their own way
out, up and ahead.

PRESERVING OCTOBER 1997

for my son

The first frosty days of fall,
the fall Grampi died, you and I lingered
at the mountain cabin of his heart
among our pots of steaming apples
picked in green and red abundance
from the neighbor orchard, the one
where you once led Grampi by the hand,
tenderly offering him samples
of firm young fruit plucked perfect and round.

We laughed and cried and stirred,
you and I, mingling memory and
the morning's task—tending the apples
we cut by hand in their passage
from crisp slices to thick tender pulp,
bubbling slowly, still slower
deepening to gold, amber and bronze.
We stirred in sugar, cinnamon and cloves,
watching closely against scorching
as the morning hours spilled beyond noon; then
spooned the fragrant apple butter into steaming jars,
sealed the lids and turned the jars
to set.

MY LITTLE GUY HAS ONE OF HIS OWN

for my son

Wasn't it just yesterday your perfect
birth progressed—water, flesh, aftermath—
and you resting on my bare breast silently
bonding our mutual lives?

Twenty-five years on the same math
repeats—breath   life   love—
one preceding then following the other.

Now you, proud Papa of your own little guy,
plump cheeks and nose so like your own
know the lines between us stretching
ahead by circling back, each of us shaped
by what came before.

THIS SMALL SINGER

for my grandson

My hopes and fears meet
in this small singer
snuggled into my neck
begging *'baby song, baby song!'*

or sprawled across my lap,
'more song, OK' nodding approval
wide as any door of hope. Myriad notes
running up scale and down, harmonies

and rounds join the balance of us
in heartfelt song no matter the season.
Song holds my hopes, met
in this small child, son of my son,

who gently strokes my head, his blue eyes
gazing right into mine, saucer size
with concern only a toddler can beam
an ancient knowing shared with the dog

to whom he patiently reads *'Ginger Boy'*
explaining its pictures
in single syllables,
charmed at having mastered

the flow of the tale, its lines a music
unto itself, rhythm and cadence lilting
through his just-learning-words speech
that rises and falls with his grasp of a phrase.

We'll stick with the hopes, thanks
to the sweet voice of request and laughter,
the sing-song renditions of spiders and rowboats
as a whole world unfolds from A to Z

through song and story by this young singer
holding my hand, and my heart.

"my hopes and fears are met/In this small singer holding onto my hand" from "December" by Gary Johnson, printed in *The Writer's Almanac*, December 22, 2011

HUNGER

Six days before he died, Dad slumped
in the gloom of the common room
where they park food
before the averse.

To brighten his spirit,
I wheeled him out to bask
in shades of scarlet maple
and reckless fuchsia
of late-blooming impatiens.

Seizing the moment, my arm,
his hunger blazed through me,
this rough-cheeked hug rare
as an autumn bud. He turned
to nuzzle my neck

making up for lost time
      or anticipating it.

PANTOUM FOR MY FATHER

In the natural progression of a life now ending,
dignified and minimizing his own frailty
as if he might walk out the door and get on with his life,
lay this man I had always known as Dad.

Dignified and minimizing his own frailty
through habit and routine inside his limitations,
this man I had always known as Dad
made me recall feelings I never had.

Habit and routine inside his limitations
offered openings through which we touched and hugged,
made me recall feelings I never had
and the truths he lived by, abundantly shared.

Openings through which we touched and hugged
around the corner of his final lap
and the truths he lived by, abundantly shared
beckoned me to honor who he had always been.

Around the corner of his final lap—
as if he might walk out the door and get on with his life—
was I beckoned to honor who he had always been
through this natural progression of a life now ending.

COURAGE

May 1996, for my daughter

One sultry summer day, we
rode bikes down off the Hill to Oak Park.
You, our able nine-year-old, fretted
about gears, your ten-speed
not yet known to you.

Part way back up, we stopped to wait.
And you, red-faced and sweaty
walked your bike, crying;
then flung it down and turned back
down the hill, singular resolve
in your hunched shoulders
*"I'm looking for something
I've lost,"* flew from your retreating back.

 Later, at home, you confided
*"I lost my courage coming up the hill;
I went back down
to find it."*

THE KEY

to my daughter on her engagement

Finding the key to your heart is not so simple
as reaching into your pocket to open the door
of home, especially

when emptiness lurks in place of the key
that would quell the panic at your plight—
outside the locked door of home, alone,
and you on the verge of tears—but not

those that spill with the deepening love
you feel for him who holds your heart
through pain and in joy, to step with you
through each door you will face, the key
to the only home you'll ever need.

FOR KEEPS

"May I keep it?" she asks,
brown eyes beseeching
as plump fingers clutch
one hard lump, the last
ashen remain of her older brother
now scattered from 'his' rock
at ocean's edge; her

heart hungering for comfort
in the face of this finality,
the familiar disintegrated
and dispersed; her innocence
seeking solace in our seaside custom
to collect, keep and not
let go.

THE RETURN

She appears, delivered down the escalator
a day late from exploring foreign lands.
Bleary-eyed, she lands in my arms
tearful, travel-weary and hungry as alone
and penniless she just navigated a flight
delayed too long to connect at midnight,
holding herself together through sheer will
and the random stranger's concern.

Her surprise tears recall how one year
earlier she hauled herself fist over arm
through felled trunks and brambles
focused homeward from a deep-woods fall
that left her ankle shattered, raw—
her tears flowing after valor,
once safely home.

She lays her head on my shoulder, her relief
a touching down on the firm ground of home
to connect, regroup, 'til she takes off again.

THE MOMENT

Father's Day 1991

I remember the moment I gave life
to my youngest, soft early
light layered through open skylight, and
in my husband's brown eyes.

I recall his intense longing,
the urgency of mine. Looking back
I see the prospect
a child might result
fueled our passion
as so often before.

And I felt the moment
new life started within.
A click in my womb,
a stirring
as sperm found egg
for the last time.

FULL CIRCLE

for my sister

Last night you lay curled
before sleep, your fragile frame
barely denting your soft bed. I massaged
your back, arms, hands, legs and feet
the way, in my early years your hand was the last
I felt before sleep soothing me into quiet,
filling holes left by an uneasy mother; holes
you, too, carried and soon enough filled
with resentment at being consigned to my care.

But last night, you sighed under my hands
oiling skin thinned with the depletions of time,
smoothing scar and keratosis, the fissured hump
of heel hard and immovable at the end
of withered calf, soaking in tenderness, time
hovering uncertainly overhead
as I held you, crooned our cradle song
*'only don't forget to sail
 back again to me'*

PRESENCE

Despite single digits outside, my temperature rises
inverse to my hope . Why do I imagine
my stubbornness trumps hers?

We are who we are, more sisters than kin.
I entice with aromas that waft through her
few rooms, garlic and cumin dancing

invitation to want, each approached
then abandoned to lost appetite.

Sitting with her prevails. Moments
pass between us. A memory flickers at the edge
of a clear-eyed gaze. We slide seamlessly

from symptoms to sorrow. She sleeps, wakes,
shuffles slowly, stops. We pass the time.
Time passes, each moment a present.

LATE SPRING

Winter's bone-gray fingers refused spring
to Vermont, holding April under icy mud
despite a few dedicated robins, cardinals' urging
and occasional young chickadee training
for anticipated mating rites ahead.

Throughout the day's drive to southern PA
rolling hills morphed to vibrant green,
redbud vivid through white blossomed clouds,
all shades of renewal surging across
both roadside and hill. Arriving

in late afternoon sun to my sister's, my eyes
accustomed to such brilliance searched
to find her emerge from her darkened room,

resolute smile cracking the façade of her
bony frame barely balanced advancing
to hug. Our shared animation belied
her slow gait, her slight weight unknown
since childhood angled sharp in my arms.

Throughout the week, we weeded the bygone
from closet and heart; plotted and planted
her deck-edge garden, its blooms feeding her
like the fragrant food and rollicking laughter
that plumped her cheeks; then dressed her

brightly from shawl to skirt,
a second spring emerging
from the dark of before.

LAUGHTER

Laughter is the great release from a too-serious self,
a burst of endorphins through the soul;
the bones of a strong sense of absurd;
the lens for balance, bright palette
against a dark day.

Laughter roots us to centuries of women
who've tunneled through torture, trauma and loss
to reach the light that cradled them,
sprouting wings to escape low-lying days
filled with pain, with want.

Laughing with women's a raucous affair,
nod to a Sisterhood known in our bones
to be holders and held through the highs, the lows;
both wing for perspective and soil to nourish
support as we spread branches
one to another, laugher making of us
one shared ground.

FALL SONG

On the rise of wind she sniffs,
leaps lithe in frosty air, shadow dance
on leaves that crunch crisp
beneath my feet—though silent
under hers.

Earthbound, yet my spirit soars
with her neon orange neck agleam
in swirling circles, entire
tree fall tumbling, twirling
as she runs, returns, fleet and frisky,
eager for each new breath; as if to swallow
autumn whole, she glides, gallops
points, returns, effortless in endless work
of play in mid-autumn woods

midway between summer's light
and winter's dark, this late afternoon
glow of setting sun settling
into calmer pace, one she's not yet
set to receive, reveling instead
in youthful vigor and delight
in autumn's edging amber light.

ZEN DOG

Short attention span,
some would say of she who can
hold my gaze as long as I ask

but flits from scent to tree
to moving hand, eager
to be the one to greet

to instigate encounters
of frolic and speed.
Throw a ball

and she runs quick as silver;
but once there, turns
to flowers, or from the child

planted there.
I've come to see
she lives 'beginner's mind'

the only one of us
truly present
moment to moment.

WORDS THE DOG KNOWS

Look, Loki! Are you ready?
Go get it—bring it here.
Good girl!!

On land this, followed by one hand
on her neck, then *give!* and her gentle
release into the other; then
the expectant upward glance,
a plea. So again I throw,
she catches or chases.
No matter, we play
until one of us
tires.

In water, she was always
game. But lately seems tired,
no longer in thrall of stick or ball
or even the bright orange tug toy
that bops goofily away with the wind.

I recognize this lessened zeal,
the loosening of her determined grip
on those endless games of her youth.
No words needed, just that look
lying between fatigue and disinterest,
with a bit of apology thrown in.

How do dogs speak so eloquently
without speech, while we use so many words
to explain away our waning interest
when so much more might be said
with a simple, soulful stare.

LIVING WITH DYING

I sit motionless as the cat's eye staring at space
where I touched his nose as he breathed his last.

I struggle to stay the sorrow
that would swallow me from tenderness—
his head rising to my fingered touch, purr
rippling his ravaged spine as I soothed
each long hour of wait.

I sit with the hole in my heart, the whole of left behind
to hold—mother, father, best friend, son—
each loss reborn spirals love beyond
what I can hold; in heart time, all loss is one.

I sit in the silence of his absent purr—
how we have lain these many nights
brow to brow, breathing as one curled
within each other's warmth in solace
and sleep—these days passed

living and dying as one.

SEEING MYSELF FOR THE FIRST TIME

I saw myself for the first time
in my husband's insistence on love
'*warts and all*,' how he looked at me

not with doe-eyed longing, surprise
nor even the closed-off sadness of want;
but how he slumped to the floor with me

my by-then soggy shirt no shield from his love,
how he held my head, and crooned—yes,
crooned—his desire for soul mate dreamed

far back as how love might look. He understood then
what took decades more for us to name:
to see and be seen for just who we are

despite warts, worries or desire. It was he
who first grasped how I nurture and tend,
urge promise to life; who blessed me with love

and saw in my eyes the life I could not,
his seeing me, after all this time
letting me see myself for the first.

COURAGE and GRACE

for my husband

When you've lived a life of grace
alight with courage and aligned with drive,
your body becomes you—athletic and lithe

in line with designs to lope along your day,
alight your steely-wheeled steed in smooth arcs
of swing and sit, saddled with little more than joy in ease.

But what happens when that body slides
into dis-ease; wobbles when you would stand fast,
slips when you would stride making you mind

each step like a small child defying
the ways of a life you wish to keep—
just enough challenge to keep you on your toes?

What if you no longer feel your toes
and your legs won't comply with desired intent?
When movement becomes awkward, then

you have embarked upon a new path
each day's *whose body have I wakened in?*
an impetus of yesterday tremoring you back under cover

wishing it would pass, knowing you must rise
and stumble across the room, right foot
dragging behind your arm hanging weak.

So you pray for renewed strength
to make of each moment
the full covenant your life has known;

absent the smooth confidence of grace,
each movement a leaning into courage
as you fumble onward the best you can.

NEW ENGLAND MEMORY

I remember the feel of bunny grass
its soft nest of warm green tickling my cheek
soaking in every ray before they dissipated
into cool shade.

I remember the stillness of my solitude
how annoyed I felt when demands shook me
from my reverie, a hand clamped
over my sense of freedom.

I forget how long I could lie there,
or why that one place was sacred, mine.

I remember the upfield apple trees
ebullient with bloom-filled armfuls
my dad would carry indoors, perfume
the air with such sweetness none could resist.

I forget why our apples never grew, or when
I learned to crave the crunch of crisp tart Macouns.

I remember summer as hot, long and languid,
the bike rides aimlessly pulling uphill and down
the meandering country roads
of Sunday afternoons with Dad.

I remember the wonderful cool
of White's Pond, how quickly it faded
walking back up the hundred steps
for the car ride home.

I remember how endless those sleepless nights
the whippoorwill's mournful moaning
pushing through the heavy dark
of bad dreams.

I forget how it all ended,
or when.

SHE AND I

Sitting by the stilled pond, I am startled
by the earnest green eyes gazing up through me
to the tall pine tree, imposing trustee
of my childhood home and innocence.

She is nine, has just learned how tender
her guileless heart toward a young kid in need,
the joy of its gamboled frolic at her
approach. She gazes skyward

never imagining herself salt-and-peppered,
awed still by the promise of nature
as in her youth. I quell an urge to touch her cheek,
the soft slope of its sadness dragging her down,
unnoticed, into 'not good enough.'
For what, I want to ask? Good enough,

I want her to see, to have lived
sixty years more emerged
from invisibility into tangible life—
our three children—whom I suddenly wish
she could befriend. I raise my own eyes
to the trees ringing the pond
none a tall pine, but grand enough

to take me back to these roots,
my natural loves twined together
like our images on the pond's surface.

DELIBERATION

Burlington, VT

Each spring I crane to first see
skinny legs sporting steely-blue
of the ancient blue heron

early to return and last to leave
this northern mountain pond
he has claimed, much as I

have claimed him great blue
totem, gauging presence
by his deliberate appearance

at the ponds of two homes.
He shies from the camera
as well he should. I see him

trust his return, whether to
seaside or mountain pond;
whether or not the same bird

he remains steadfast in presence
as does my belief in him.

DISCOVERY

The path of discoveries
forks ever wider. The more
I think I know, the greater
the choice and less I am sure.

We grow through uncertainty
and the urge to keep moving
to keep ourselves whole

perhaps to discover we might
be driven by reasons neither noble
nor true. Yet the unknown

opens prospects;
and while clarity may ensue,
it's the wandering that teaches,
the open heart that receives.

Like an itinerant beggar
bowl in hand let me lean
into the space where questions sleep

questions I never knew I had,
and need not hold
nor answer

but simply walk into
unafraid, receiving
what falls into my bowl

for the gift it is
letting assumptions
        fall
                away.

FOUND

She is not the one left
holding the family center
at the threshold
she strives to honor, the one shifting
across years and intransigencies
of family need.

No, she is the one standing tall
her own center firmly planted in heart
and feet that step her own way.

You will know her.
She strides
unapologetic and strong
from the shadow
into a circle of women.

She speaks her name.
She is not lost.

EQUINOX

Her eyes, like tunnels, burrow through
layered time, parsing and parting
eons, excavating words unspoken

and adventures dreamed as real
as the outgrowths and implosions of spirit
that define one's passage across the years.

If you look, you will find
the shape of yourself separating slowly
from what you thought you knew, leaving

it all behind as mulch to nurture
those yet to come, the whole of your life
dancing like a river ever onward

casting on, casting off, cycling
to return form unto form, as life itself
rises and falls on the updrafts and channels
of inevitable change.

Sarah W. Bartlett was greatly influenced by her father, a world-class chemist devoted to making the world a better place. From him she learned the value of community and a love of words at play. Sarah spent the first 25 years of her professional life using language in service to planning, marketing and public relations for non profit organizations.

In 1993, she first participated in *Women Writing for (a) Change*®, where she quickly embraced the life-altering power of sharing story within a mirroring community of women. By 2004 she had become licensed to found *Women Writing for (a) Change—Vermont. LLC*. In 2010, she founded *writing inside VT*, a weekly writing group inside Vermont's sole women's prison using the same intentional practices to encourage healing writing for personal and social change within a supportive community. Now in its eighth year, the program hosts an active blog (www.writinginsideVT.com) and continues to hold readings and book talks based on the 2013 publication of HEAR ME, SEE ME: INCARCERATED WOMEN WRITE (Orbis Books), which Sarah co-edited. She has published a number of pieces and delivered two keynote speeches about this work.

Sarah's current work as change agent and poet draws on the full range of her experience and prior training, including a doctorate in health education from Harvard. Her professional publications comprise contributions to respected academic journals. Her poetry and prose has appeared in *Adanna, the Aurorean, Minerva Rising, PoemMemoirStory, Mom Egg Review, Ars Medica*; and highly-acclaimed anthologies, including the award-winning WOMEN ON POETRY (McFarland & Co. Inc., 2012). Her first poetry chapbook was INTO THE GREAT BLUE: MEDITATIONS OF SUMMER (Finishing Line Press, 2011).

Language remains the medium for her dual life work: creating communities that support individual transformation and healing, and her own creative writing. She does not know how to live without pen in hand. Like the hummingbird who has taught her to see deep into the heart of things, she seeks to awaken the soul to presence.

Her reflections on both external and interior worlds draw on family and her homes in the Vermont mountains and Massachusetts shore, where she lives with her husband and pets.

www.ingramcontent.com/pod-product-compliance
Lightning Source LLC
LaVergne TN
LVHW041508070426
835507LV00012B/1418